Jubilate

Bob Chilcott

for soprano or tenor solo, SATB chorus, and brass ensemble or piano

Vocal score

MUSIC DEPARTMENT

OXFORD
UNIVERSITY PRESS

OXFORD
UNIVERSITY PRESS

Great Clarendon Street, Oxford OX2 6DP, England
198 Madison Avenue, New York, NY10016, USA

Oxford University Press is a department of the University of Oxford.
It furthers the University's aim of excellence in research, scholarship,
and education by publishing worldwide in

Oxford New York
Auckland Bangkok Buenos Aires Cape Town Chennai
Dar es Salaam Delhi Hong Kong Istanbul Karachi Kolkata
Kuala Lumpur Madrid Melbourne Mexico City Mumbai Nairobi
São Paulo Shanghai Taipei Tokyo Toronto

Oxford is a registered trade mark of Oxford University Press
in the UK and in certain other countries

First published 1999

19

ISBN 978-0-19-355827-4

Music origination by
Barnes Music Engraving Ltd., East Sussex.
Printed in Great Britain on acid-free paper by
Halstan & Co. Ltd., Amersham, Bucks.

Jubilate is scored for Soprano or Tenor solo, SATB chorus,
2 Horns in F, 3 Trumpets in B♭, 3 Trombones,
Tuba, Timpani, and Piano solo.

Orchestral material is available for hire
from the publisher's hire library.

Duration: *c.*16 minutes

Dedicated to Simon Carrington and the University of Kansas Chamber Choir
Commissioned by Helen and Walter Crockett and the KU Department of Music and Dance

Jubilate

O be joyful

Book of Common Prayer

BOB CHILCOTT

Printed in Great Britain

OXFORD UNIVERSITY PRESS, MUSIC DEPARTMENT, GREAT CLARENDON STREET, OXFORD OX2 6DP

9
S.
A.
(unis.) p dolce
O be joy - ful,
TENOR & BASS unis. p dolce
T.
B.
O be joy - ful,
12
be joy - ful in the Lord,
be joy - ful
15
mp
all ye lands:
serve the Lord, the
serve the Lord
serve the Lord, the
mp
mp

18
Lord
with glad - ness,
serve the
Lord
21
serve the Lord, the Lord
Lord
with glad - ness,
serve the Lord, the Lord
24
mp cresc.
and come be - fore his
mp cresc.

26
mp cresc.
and come be - fore his pre - sence with a
mp cresc.
pre - sence with a song, a song, cresc. and
29
cresc.
song, a song, and come be - fore his
come be - fore his pre - sence with a song, a
cresc.
32
f
pre - sence with a song, a
song,
f
f

34
dim.
song,
a
song,
a
dim.
dim.
36
dolce
song,
a
song.
dolce
dolce
38
rit.
rit.
dim.
p
pp

Gerard Manley Hopkins

*Song

* For liturgical performances a cut may be made from the end of bar 45 to bar 120 (page 12) where the Jubilate text continues with 'Be ye sure'.

57
poco stringendo
mp cresc.
Once I turned from thee and hid, Bound on what thou hast for-bid; Sow the wind I would; I
mp cresc.
f
60
dim. e rit.
a tempo
p
sinned: I re - pent of what I did. Bad I am, but yet thy child.
p
64
Fa-ther, be thou re-con-ciled. Spare thou me, since I see With thy might that thou art mild.
(R.H.)
68
poco stringendo
mp cresc.
I have life left with me still And thy pur-pose to ful-fil; Yea a debt to pay thee yet:
mp cresc.
f

71
rit.
dim.
a tempo
p
cresc.
Help me, sir, and so I will. But thou bidst, and just thou art, Me shew
dim.
p
75
mer-cy from my heart To-wards my bro-ther, ev-'ry o-ther Man my mate and coun-ter-part,
cresc.
78
dim. e rit.
3
a tempo
To-wards my bro-ther, ev-'ry o-ther Man my mate and coun-ter-part.
p
82
S.
A.
SOPRANO
p espress.
ALTO
Thee, God, I come from, to thee
TENOR
T.
B.
BASS
p espress.
pp

86
All day
poco cresc.
go,
long I like fountain flow
From thy hand out swayed a-bout
poco cresc.
poco cresc.
89
dim.
p
As ac-
poco cresc.
Mote-like in thy might-y glow.
What I know of thee I bless,
dim.
p
poco cresc.
93
-know-ledg-ing thy stress On my be-ing and as see-ing Some-thing of thy ho-li-ness.
poco cresc.

96
poco stringendo
Yea a debt to
mf f
mp cresc.
I have life left with me still; to pay thee yet:
mp cresc.
mp cresc.
mf f
I have life left with me still And thy pur-pose to ful-fil; Yea a debt to
poco stringendo
mp cresc.
f
99
rit.
mp dim.
a tempo
p
Me shew
cresc.
Help me, sir, and so I will. But thou bidst, and just thou art,
mp dim.
p
cresc.
rit.
a tempo
dim.
p
103
mer-cy from my heart To-wards my bro-ther, ev-'ry o-ther Man my mate and coun-ter-part,
p cresc.

106
dim.
dim. e rit.
a tempo
To-wards my bro-ther, ev-'ry o-ther Man my mate and coun-ter-part.
dim.
dim. e rit.
a tempo
espress.
p
110
SOPRANO (or TENOR) SOLO
p
Thee, God, I come from, to thee
p
Thee, God, I come from, to thee
p
pp
114
mp
go, to thee go.
mp
go, go.
mp
p

Be ye sure

120
Rhythmic and bright ♩ = c.168
f
ff

124
S.
A.
T.
B.
f
Be ye sure that the Lord he is God,

129
f
Be ye sure that the Lord
ff

133
ff
he is God,
ff
f
ff
137
ff
that the Lord he is God, that the Lord he
ff
sfz
141
f
is God: it is he that hath made us, it is he that hath made us,
f
sfz
f

(♩ = ♩)
ff
146
and not we our - selves.
our - selves.
ff
dim.
and, and not we our - selves, not we our - selves.
(♩ = ♩)
ff
dim.
f dim.
mp
p dolce
154
(Tpt. solo)
mp cantabile
160
167
mf
cresc.
mp

174
mp
dim.
180
p
187
p espress.
S.
A.
We are his peo - ple, and the sheep of his pas -
T.
B.
p espress.
mp espress.
193
mp espress.
- ture. We are his peo - ple, and the
mp espress.

199
We are his peo -
mp espress.
sheep of his pas - ture.
We
mp
mp
205
- ple,
we
We are his peo - ple,
are his peo - ple,
mp
We are his peo -
are his peo - ple,
211
dim. poco a poco
we are his
we are his peo - ple,
dim. poco a poco
- ple,
dim. poco a poco

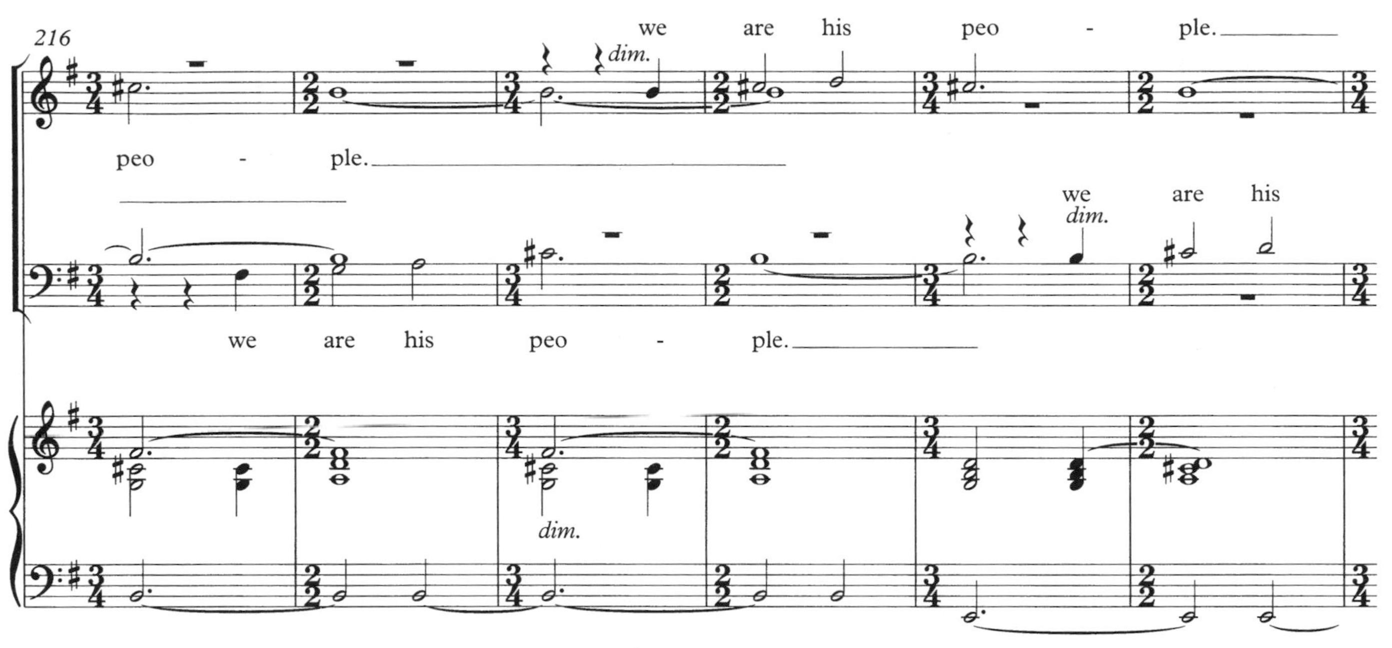

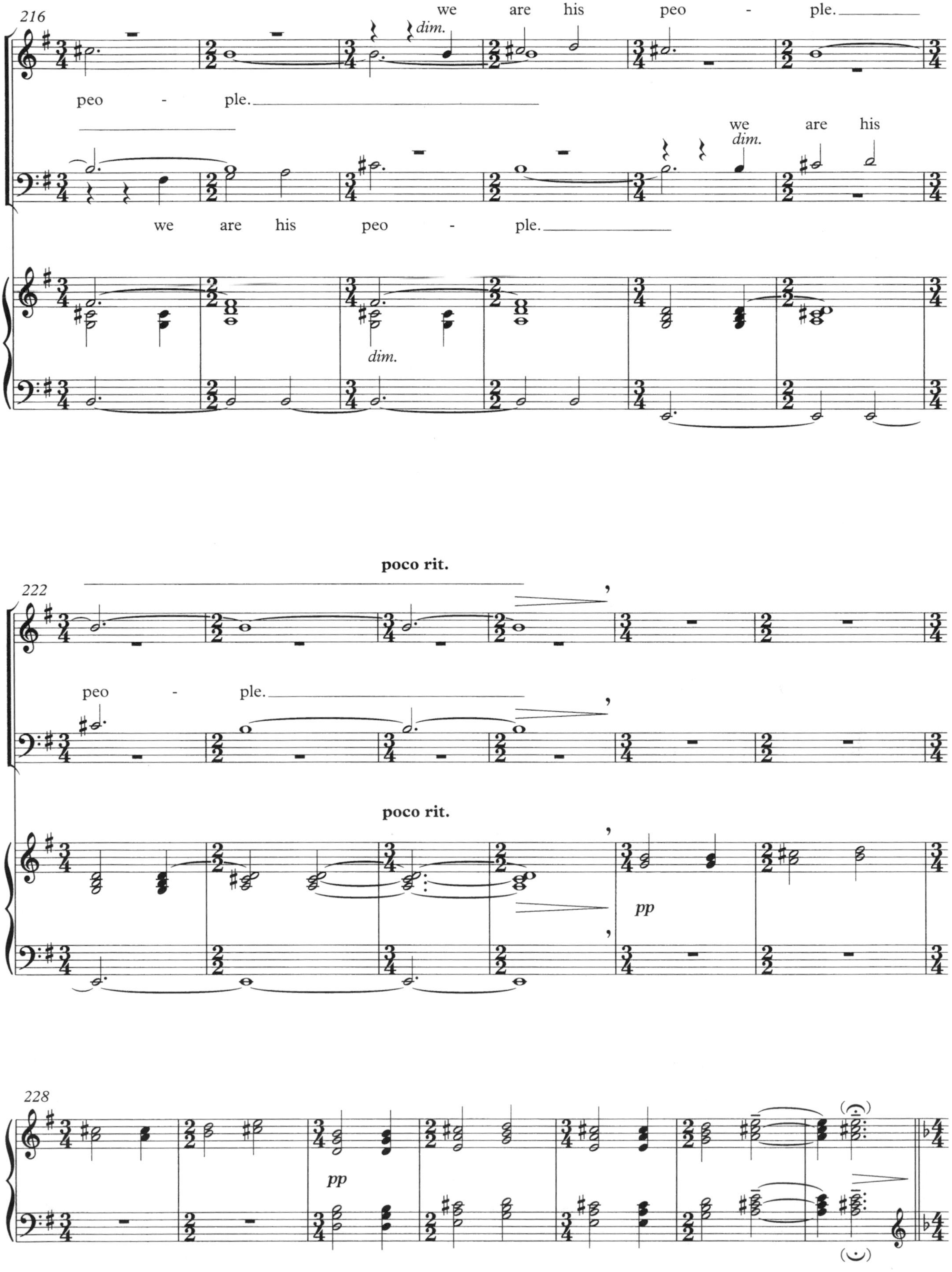

222

poco rit.

peo - ple.

poco rit.

pp

228

pp

O go your way

Like a fanfare ♩ = c.96
235
239
244
S.1
A.
O go your way in-to his gates with thanks-giv - ing,
O go your way,
247
S.2
O go your way in-to his gates with thanks-giv - ing,

250
p marcato
T.
and in - to his courts with praise, and in - to his courts, his
p marcato
B.
and in - to his courts with praise, and in - to his courts, his
p
253
SOPRANO 1
S.1
Go your way in - to his gates with thanks -
ALTO
A.
way,
T.
courts with praise,
B.
courts with praise,
f
258
S.1
- giv - ing, go your way in - to his gates with thanks -
SOPRANO 2
S.2
Go your way in - to his
A.
way, way,
(R.H.)

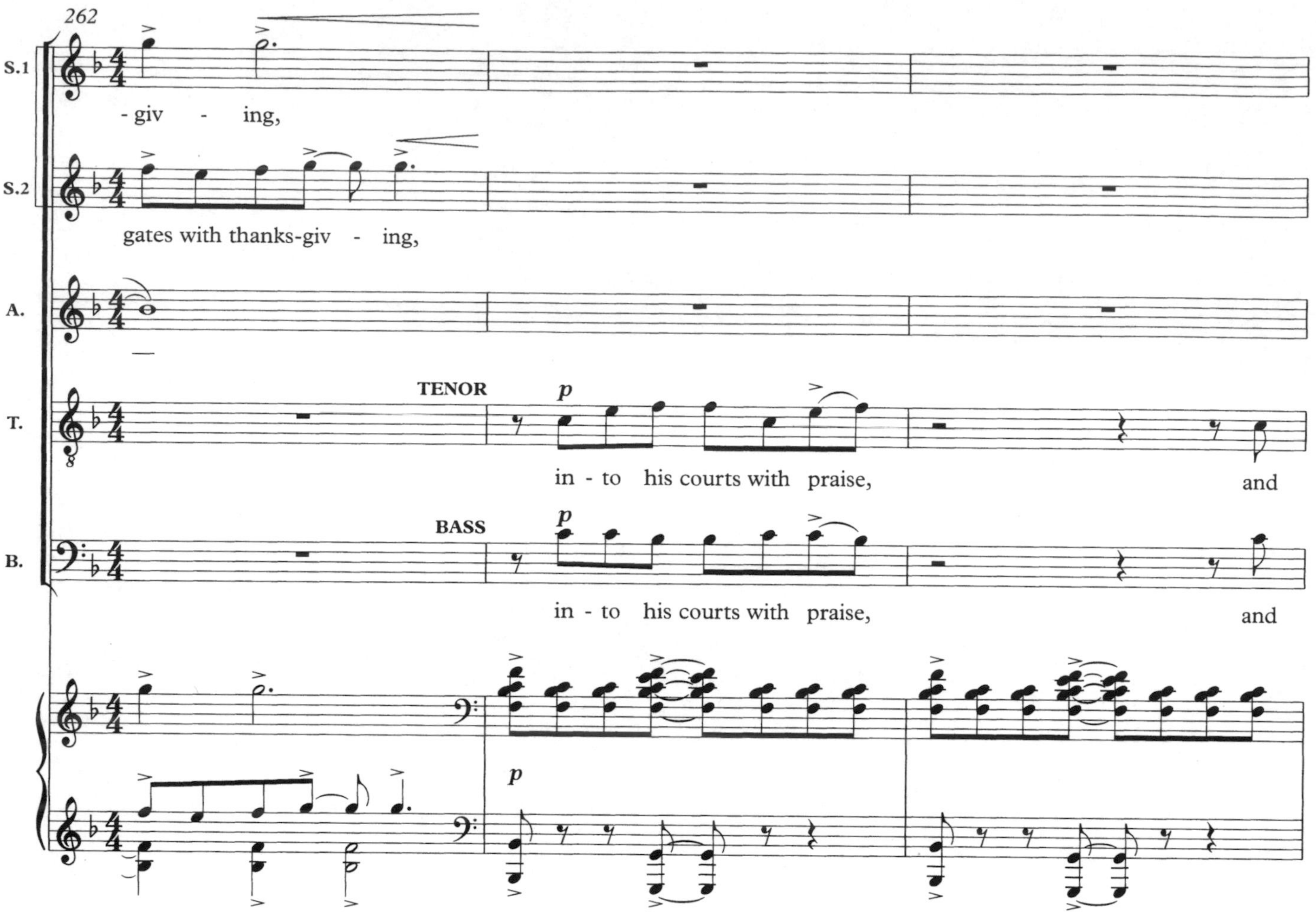
262
S.1
-giv - ing,
S.2
gates with thanks-giv - ing,
A.
TENOR
T.
p
in - to his courts with praise,
and
BASS
B.
p
in - to his courts with praise,
and
p

265
A.
p cresc.
go, go your way,
T.
cresc.
in - to his courts with_ praise, with_ praise,___ in - to his courts with praise,
B.
cresc.
in - to his courts with_ praise, with_ praise,___ in - to his courts with praise,
cresc.

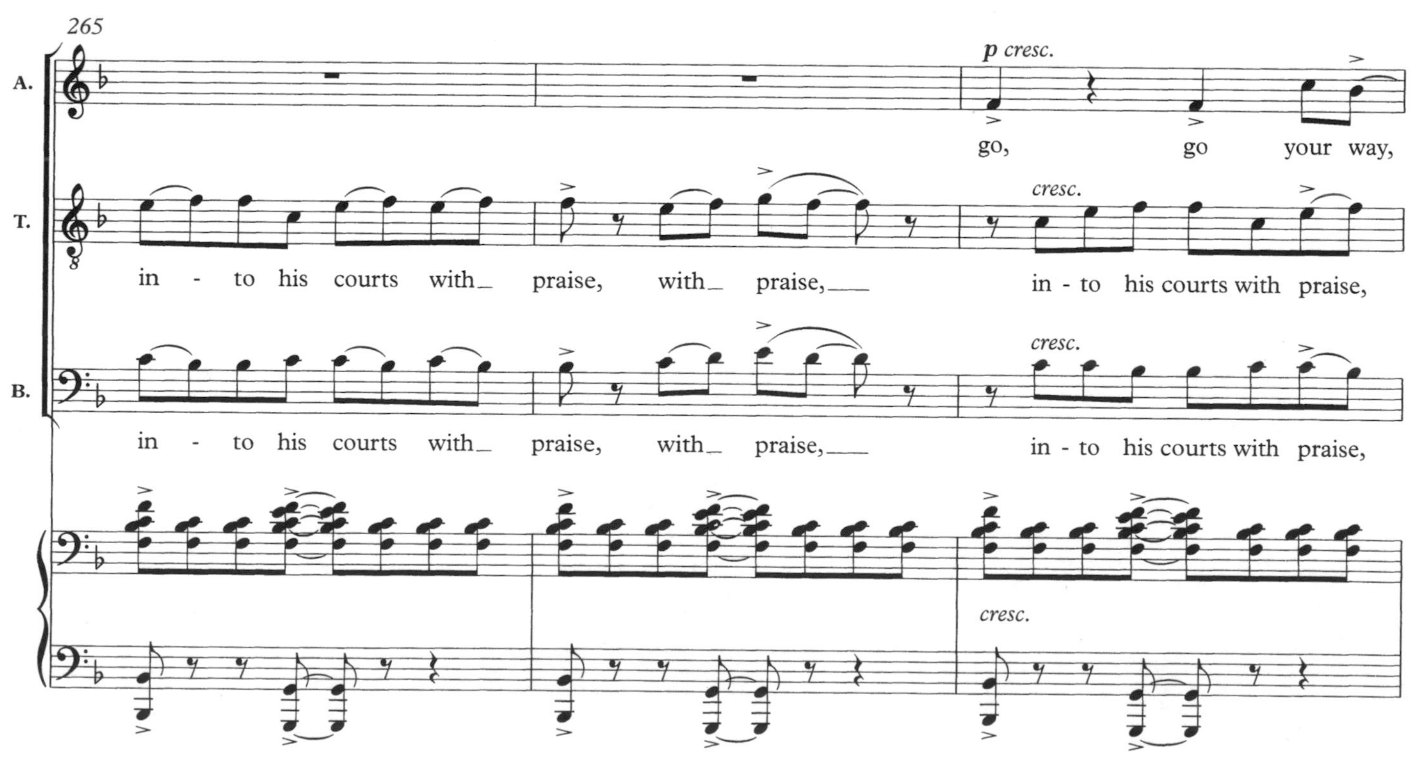

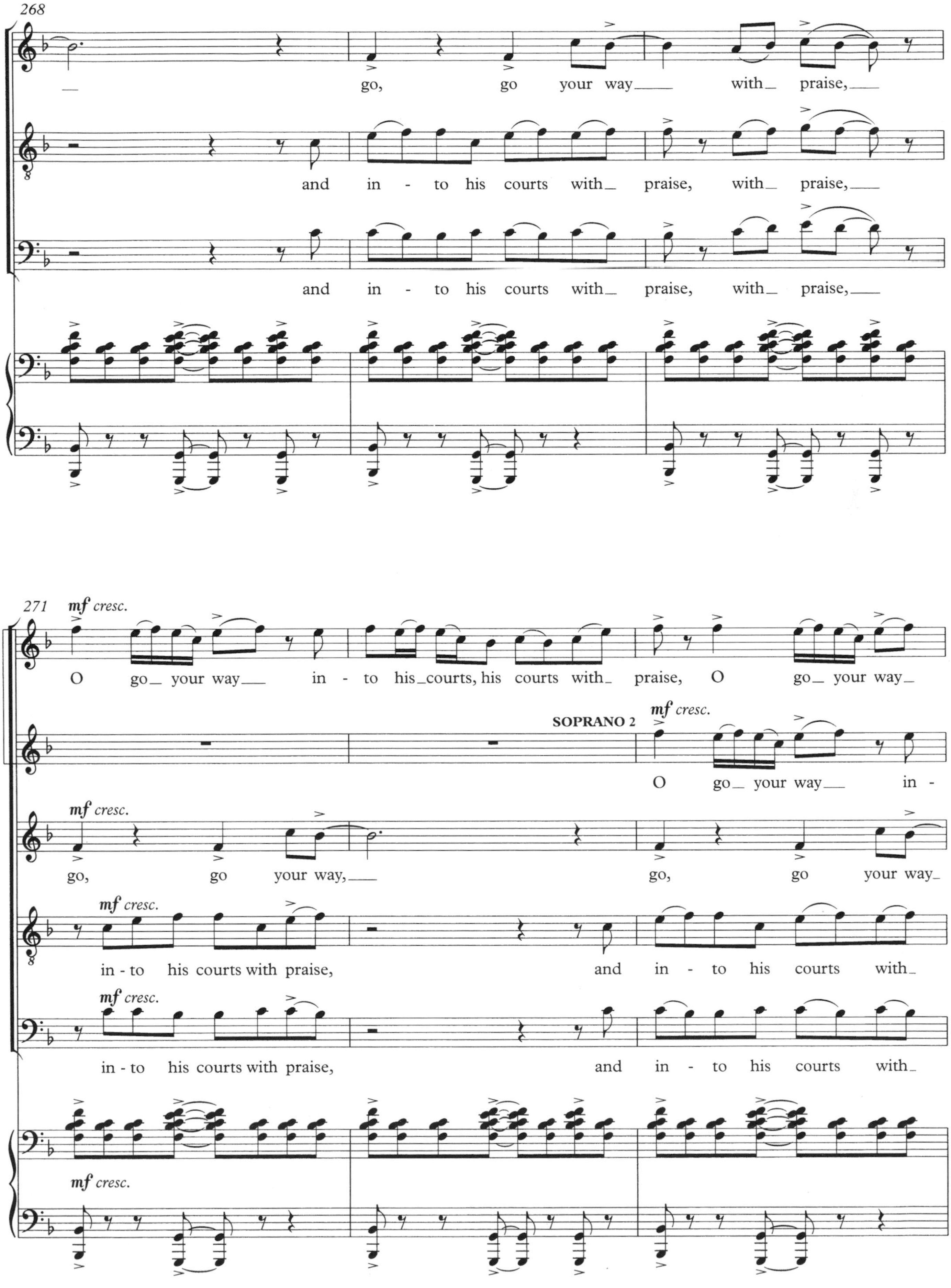

271

S.1 *mf cresc.*
O go your way in - to his courts, his courts with praise, O go your way

S.2 SOPRANO 2 *mf cresc.*
O go your way in -

A. *mf cresc.*
go, go your way, go, go your way

T. *mf cresc.*
in - to his courts with praise, and in - to his courts with

B. *mf cresc.*
in - to his courts with praise, and in - to his courts with

mf cresc.

274
cresc.
in - to his _ courts, his courts with _ praise, with _ praise, with _ praise, with _ praise.
ff
- to his _ courts, his courts _ with _ praise, with _ praise, with _ praise, with _ praise.
— with __ praise, __ with _ praise, with _ praise, _ with _ praise.
praise, with __ praise, __ with _ praise, with _ praise, _ with _ praise.
praise, with __ praise, __ with _ praise, with _ praise, _ with _ praise.
277
f
281
p

Be thankful

Broad ♩ = c.76
286
S.
A.
SOPRANO & ALTO unis.
p dolce e legato
Be thank - ful,
p dolce

289
be thank - ful,
be thank - ful

292
un - to him,

295
S.
A.
(unis.) p dolce
be thank - ful, be
T.
B.
unis. p dolce
Be thank - ful,
298
thank - ful, be
be thank - ful,
300
mp
thank - ful
un - to him, to
un - to him,
mp
un - to him, to
mp

303
him,
be thank - ful
un - to
him,
306
un - to him, to him,
him,
be
un - to him, to him,
308
thank - ful,
mp cresc.
and speak
mp cresc.

311
mp cresc.
and speak good of his
mp cresc.
good of his name, his name,
314
name, his name,
cresc.
and speak good of his
cresc.
316
f
and speak good of his name, his
f
name, his name, his name, his
f

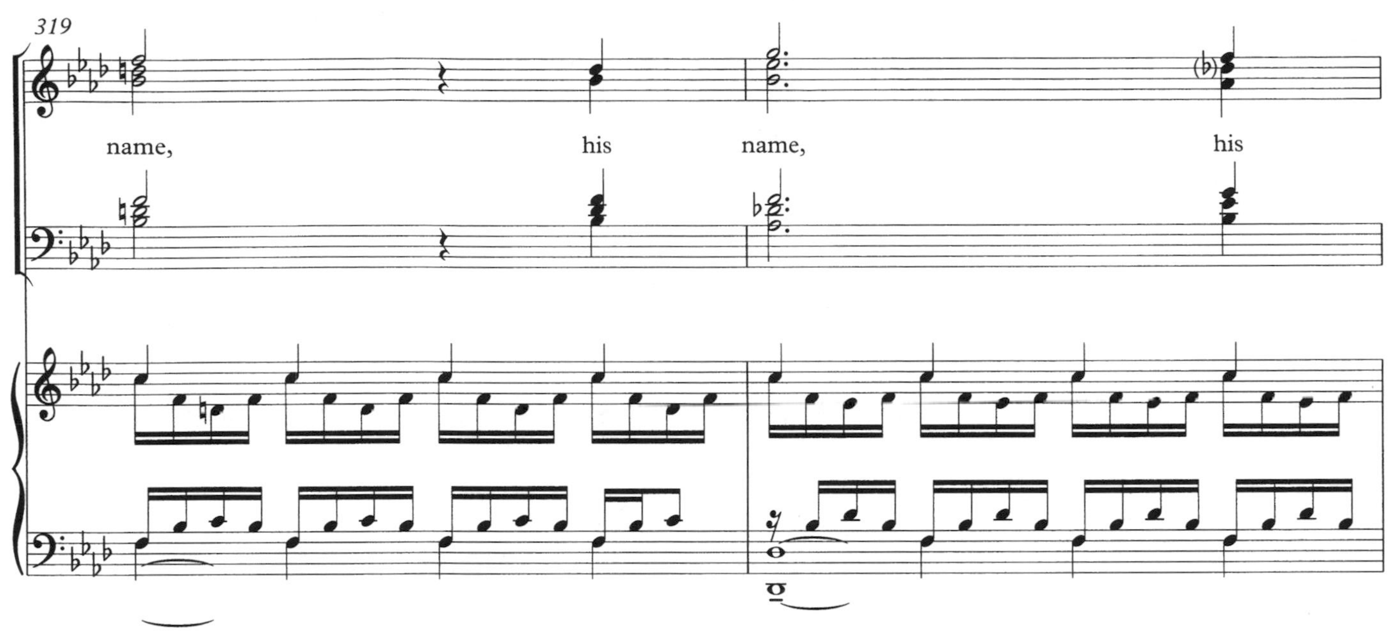
319
name,
his
name,
his

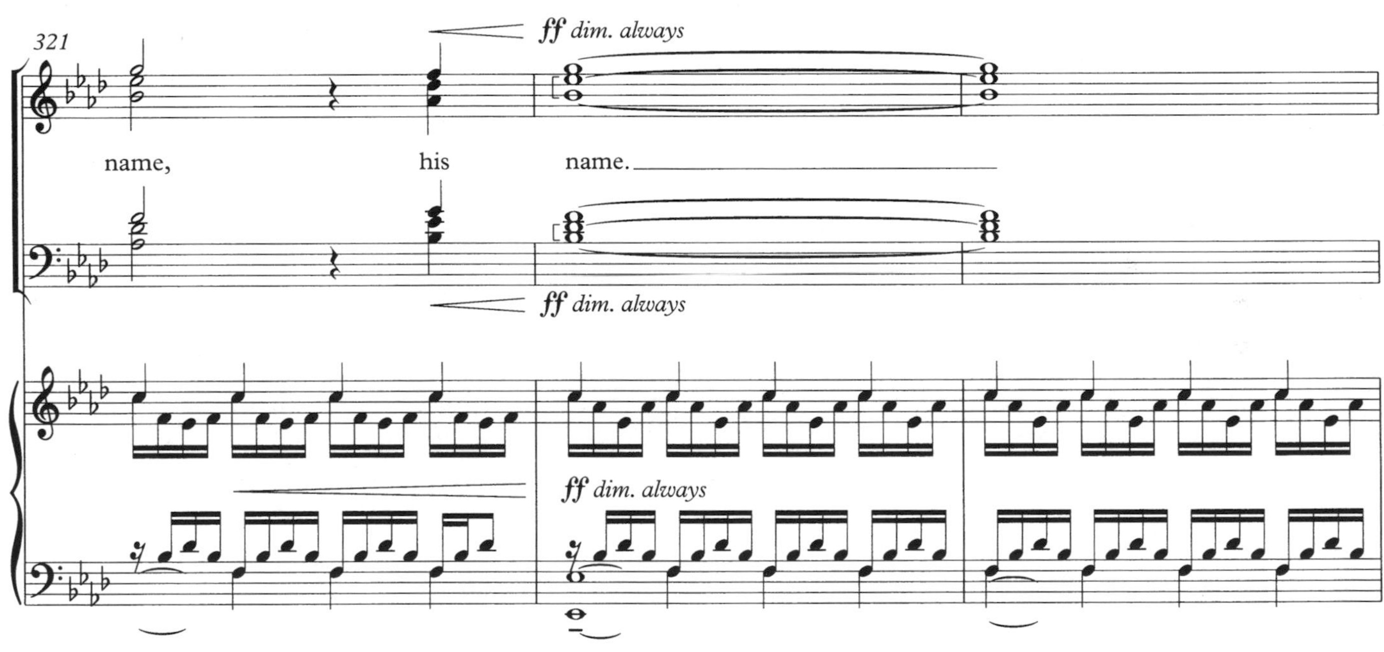
321
ff dim. always
name,
his
name.
ff dim. always
ff dim. always

324
p
pp
p

For the Lord is gracious

* For liturgical performances a plainsong Gloria Patri should be sung.